GOTTA BE
A BETTER WAY

Volume 1

Poems by

Sandréa Flowers

Release The Ink Publishing®

First Edition: May 2023

ISBN 978-0-9975600-4-6 (eBook)

ISBN 978-0-9975600-5-3 (Paperback)

Release The Ink Publishing

5.5 x 8.5"

Printed in the United States of America

Gotta Be
a Better Way

Volume 1

TABLE OF CONTENTS

The poems to come are for you and for me – those of us on this employee rollercoaster ride that ebbs and flows at a moment's notice. Those of us that are the creative and disciplined light that pushes through and stays the course.

See yourself and the thread of commonality woven through each poem – a commonality we share, whether we live in NYC, Atlanta, or Seattle, Washington. It is my hope that I've captured the voice of the voiceless – a cathartic outlet and collection of what is and what will be.

SECTION I

BEARS REPEATING

PUSH THROUGH IT

Are you tired?
Can't seem to get a handle on things?
Feeling listless and can't be bothered with anything?
Push through it!

Family and the job working your nerves,
Finding yourself constantly immersed with them
In a consciousness of chaos?
Experiencing an emotional crisis of identity and self-worth?
Push through it!

Disappointed and disturbed by the relationship
You have with food and your body?
Fighting the inclination to
Fall
Into that deep abyss of depression?
Push through it!

Yes, PUSH:
Pray, Persevere, Practice, Press on
Until
Something
Happens

Push through it!

WHY BOTHER?

Sending emails for what
when you don't even read them

Sending emails for what
when I can't even save the important ones
because you're too cheap to invest
in topnotch data storage for the files

Sending emails for what
when the receiver is only going to answer
one thing when I sent them 10 issues and concerns

Sending emails for what
when the receiver is going to respond
emotionally and not professionally
because they have an eggshell ego

Sending emails for what
when the response is going to
magnify my irritation
with all the misspelled words
and grammar and punctuation errors
I have to read through

Sending emails for what
when absolutely nothing is going to change

Why bother?

because the minute you don't
is when you're going to need it

because if it isn't written down
it didn't happen

That's why!

I AM

I AM free

Free from past learnings
(my mistakes)

Free from distraction
(what the person next to me is doing)

Free from failure
(because I have pragmatically adjusted
my actions and expectations)

I AM full

Full of gratitude
(for the choices I have made)

Full of intent
(because I never want time to be my enemy)

Full of hustle
(because I have way more to give)

I AM focused

Focused on my next best season

Focused on what matters

Focused on my family

I AM free

I AM full

I AM focused

I AM

THAT ONE BRIGHT SPOT

That one bright spot is you

That one bright spot is when I see you

That one bright spot is when
We're in our constant flow
Of walking, talking, and working

You are fun and funny
You make me WANT to like people

The goodness of your heart shows
In every word and deed.
In the belly of the beast,
You are a beautiful gift
That keeps on giving.
You are a true ride or die - that
One
Bright
Spot

YOU LIKE IT I LOVE IT

We're going to repackage and repurpose this program
That didn't work the last 5 tries

You like it. I love it.

We're going to use our back channel, hidden job market
To establish this new group
And place who we want in there
(Qualifications and competence be damned!)

You like it. I love it.

We're going to ignore the incessant pink elephants
That sashay into every meeting, lit cigarette in hand
Setting up shop

You like it. I love it.

We're going to pile on the already existing top-heavy hierarchy
Of managers and executives
You know -- you can never have too many chiefs

You like it. I love it.

We are going to champion being devoid
Of all business and common sense

You like it. I love it!

LABOR OF LOVE

When you're laboring at a labor of love
You will find the time

When you're laboring at a labor of love
You will find the energy

When you're laboring at a labor of love
You will find the space

There is no person, place, or thing
That can distance you from . . .
Your labor of love

WHAT YOU DO WHAT YOU SAY

What you do under the rock
What you do behind closed doors
What you do in the presence
Of your inner circle . . .

What you say in jest
What you say backhandedly
What you say cleverly
With scumbag undertones . . .

Doesn't matter
Because you
Did all those things
Behind my back

There is no need
For me
To give them a second thought
As I am not supposed to know

Nevertheless
I am out here
Staying breezy
Handling my business
Living my life like it's golden

SECTION II

EBB AND FLOW

THOUGHTS, SHORT & SWEET

the duality of
life and death
unbothered and stirred up
contrite and indifferent

stiff competition in tow
often sharing
the same caustic space

the many levels and layers
of
the human race

IS IT JUST ME?

The bushwa and fakery is at an all-time high today
The disingenuous kudos, atta-boys, and pats on the back
Are showing just how skillful the ones spewing them are

Heck, I thought it was just me
Thinker of one
But before I could say anything
He shared the same sentiment
When all was said and done

Is it just me?

Just put lipstick on it
Never wanting to address
Spinning our wheels
As I finally acquiesce

BORED OUT OF MY MIND

Boredom on the brink of frustration
Diametrically opposed to
The 'take it easy' ideology
Permeating these halls
The lack of brilliance
The lack of energy
The lack of progressive thought

Some take
The easy-breezy mundane conveyor belt
Of job activities, and
Their equally vacuous individual contribution
And pat themselves on the back
(All in a day's work?)

I see
The pseudo-progressive posturing
And dead-end tasks
As an affront to the path ahead
A path illuminated
And brimming with promise
Positive provocation and opportunity
Alas, I must hold on

But –

While I wait
Patiently to get there
I want nothing more
Than to drive a paperclip through my eyeball
Blood and trauma all the same
Perhaps then, I can get some excitement
Some unconventionalism
In this otherwise sterile, yester-century environment
Frozen in time

Can you tell I am bored out of my mind?
The pink elephant is in the room
Everyone keeps on keeping on
Until the next show of insincerity

NOT TO BE CONFUSED WITH . . .

Don't let the truth of my expressions
Fool you
The chaos and craziness serve a purpose
And I love it!

My pen hasn't stopped since I got here
The malleability of this place
Has brought me here
Ripe for the taking

Knowing that there are others
Experiencing the same level of consciousness
But still trekking through
Past the distractions

What's the point?
Take what by all accounts
Appears to be garbage -
Unusable and dark
And turn it into something
That allows you to
Create, enjoy, and embark

On a journey that no employee experience
Could ever give you

Because
We
Were meant
To do
And be
More
Than just
An employee

LEGACY

Talk to the mediocre employee
Man or woman
And they'll look at you with a blank stare
When you attempt to discuss legacy

Most people just go through the motions of life
Folks already dead
Just don't know it yet
Actual dead man walking

When you talk about legacy
Long-lasting impact
Passing on intangible richness and power
Being of service
In perpetuity
To more than those you are comfortable with
It goes right over their heads

So, what you do instead
Is find your audience
Find your tribe
Those that have a compatible voice
A matching vibe

Those who know there's more
Than just this here fishbowl
Leaving those other folks alone
As you
Tackle milestone after milestone

All with a view to your legacy!

THE SENSES

The smell of ambition
Sprinkled with
Cautious reservation

The touch of accessibility
Marred by cynicism

The deafening sound
Of pride and admiration
Backdoored by
Clandestine malice and doubt

The taste of purpose
Making sure of
The more important things
Coupled with temporary moments
Of uneasiness and gridlock

The sight of success
Through life's full view mirror
Taking in moments
Meaning and memories

5 senses
The impressions of which
Living, laughing, and laboring
It dispenses

WE ARE NOT THE SAME

You
Have a narrow mindset

You
Operate from a place
Of scarcity

I
Have an unlimited mindset

I
Operate from a place
Of abundance

We
Are not the same

We
Are not even in the same zip code

TRUTH NEVER GOES OUT OF STYLE

We love the fashion
Of mundane things
No real value
Flighty
Fleeting

With the lukewarm, truth ebbs and flows
As they follow what's trendy

But for the tried and true
Truth
Is a timeless classic they wear
Proudly

Truth
Delightfully sharp and palpable
Never goes out of style

The woven fabric and matching accessories
Of facts
Honesty
Justice
Staples that all of us should keep
In our moral wardrobe

As truth –
Truth NEVER goes out of style

UNSEEN

Amid complexity and chaos
You will get
Lost in the shuffle
If you do not have
That *oomph!*
To stand out

That je ne sais quoi
To captivate the masses

CRISIS IN CHARACTER

Last week
You couldn't care less
If I had something to eat or drink

Today
You vow and shout from the rooftops:
"No New Yorker will go hungry during this crisis"!

I guess
During non-crisis times
You take a 'no big deal' approach
For hungry people like me

Last month
There was no thought or concern
Of my struggle making ends meet
Being self-employed
Raising two children

Today
You're providing 3 meals a day
Opening up unemployment benefits
And health insurance options
That would otherwise not be available
To me

On end
Prior to this crisis
You flooded the airwaves and television screens
With countless influencers and messaging
On how to self-indulge
And buy, buy, buy

Today
I am bombarded with messaging
About love
Getting through this together
And health
And wellness

Crisis in character

Does the crisis reveal the character?
Or does the character reveal the crisis?

THIS PLACE IS . . .

a
veritable
romper room
and
smorgasbord
of
inequity
inefficiency
and
stupidity

HELL HATH, NO FURY

they say there's no greater fury
than that of a woman
scorned by a man
but, yes
why, yes there is
namely
that of a competent, qualified woman
passed over for promotion
in what feels like
perpetuity

where the arrow
of consideration and selection
lands on the lesser qualified
good-for-little employee
that one person content to be
happy even
acting and playing
the forever supporting role

the fury, however
redirected ferociously
focused elsewhere

EMPLOYEE OF THE YEAR

Unhinged
Drunk
On chaos, catfighting, and craziness

Think this is specific to just women?
Nope!

The men are some of the biggest folks
Flying off the rails

It's a contest to see
Who can be dirt bag of the year
The top dog
The absolute train wreck, if you will

Then there are the runners up
Train wrecks about to happen

Fascinating to watch from the bleachers
But you can't tell these fragile-ego creatures
That this is a contest
No one wins

NO WORDS

[Blank]

[Blank]

[Blank]

[Blank]

There are just no words!

[Giving a voice to indescribable feelings, "No Words" conveys the unspeakable response to many events and experiences that one encounters in their life and at their place of employment.]

ABSURDITY QUESTIONED

Everything and nothing
A forgone conclusion
Collective and indivisible
Just an illusion?

One glance one look
Very possibly many more
Absurdity du jour
From the ceiling to the floor

BAD DECISIONS

Being held hostage by bad leadership feels like a harrowing episode of *Law & Order: SVU*. Our freedom is gone and we're stuck in constant intellectual and emotional anguish, not knowing if we're going to make it out alive, and not knowing how much more we can take.

When not wanting everyone to know that you made a bad decision far outweighs removing those bad decisions so the organization can get back on track and thrive, that's when you know the priorities are topsy turvy. It becomes clear that it has never been about effective change, but rather about shuffling papers vigorously and long enough to look as if you are doing your darndest to improve things.

All the while, hoping and praying that the clock runs out as you kick the can down the road. Because everyone knows there is a 2-year shelf life with these positions — 3 years if you're [un]fortunate enough.

TIME TO RETIRE

You didn't make this decision
They made it for you
And while you've resigned yourself
After having gone through
Those 7 stages of grief
The deepest parts of you still wonder:
"Why didn't they renew my contract"?

Perhaps it's
The non-represented labor costs
You managed to increase
In a few short years
Even though productivity
Made a case to the contrary

Or

Perhaps it's
The countless times
You were unable to contribute
To the many progressive conversations
Without first consulting your handlers
Or reading your notes

Regardless

YES

It's time to retire!

THE SOIL

Put me in the right soil
And I will take you and your business
To new heights
Right processes
Right reasoning
Right programs

Beyonce said:
"Your dynasty ain't complete without a chief like me"

Conversely

Put me in bad soil
And . . . well . . .
I will sit there
And pen your days of infamy

ABSORBED IN HOPE

Better days ahead
We work through
And walk through the fear
Chaos
Uncertainty

The passing of time
Giving us Perspective
Wisdom
Clarity

We forge ahead
In our complete suit of armor
Answering the call
Staying the course
Leveling this Petri dish of a playing field

Giving this disease the gravity it deserves
We respond
With positive reinforcement
High levels of productivity
Measured compassion

Always returning to our first thought
That better days are ahead
Looking past death and despair
We anxiously wait
Living on hope and a prayer!

GIVING ME LIFE

Anita Baker and Luther Vandross make everything alright. And when it's a particularly jarring day, Jimmy Cliff, George Benson, and Boney James knock it out of the park.

Music soothes the soul beyond measure. It gives life to the overworked and underpaid.

You can almost hear Anita Baker singing, Giving You the Best That I Got, can't you?

If the words and the melody don't put your mind at ease after a hard day's work, I don't know what will.

Music gives me life!

The harmony, the rhythm the perfectly arranged tones and composition.

Had a not-so-good day? Throw on your favorites and watch the music give you life.

THERE'S ALWAYS ONE

When you come across a group
Of accomplished and well put together ladies
You can only feel a strong sense of pride
So much so that you can confidently proclaim
"Yes, those are my people!"

But is it just me?
Or is there always one in the group
Where you scratch your head wondering
"How the heck did *she* get in here?"

You know the one
A nice person
But can't help anybody, and
Really doesn't contribute
Anything of substance
To the group's advancement

The one who
When not in the presence of the tribe
Falls to pieces
Gives the store away
Acts certifiably crazy when the pressure is on

The dichotomy between this person
And the group as a whole
Is fascinating

Yes
There is *always* one!

RETICENCE

My reticence
Is a protection
As a mother is
To her newborn baby

WHAT EXACTLY ARE YOU PAYING FOR?

What am I paying for
If you all are in bed together?
No
Not that physical manifestation
Your brain immediately went to
The one where you cooperate unconditionally
At the expense of us members
And the unit as a whole

When did this deviant behavior become a social norm?
This is definitely not your dad's union
Way back when, they were a force to be reckoned with
Today, their strength is negligible, self-serving

They are definitely out for self
Ignoring those at the bottom of the ladder
Just enough
So as not to lose their control
Or upset the apple cart of privilege

Somebody help me out here

What, Exactly, Are You Paying For?

TAKE THAT TO THE BANK

It's weird to be in the thick of things at work and witness people who believe in a higher power, people who don't, and people who think *THEY* are the higher power.

He said it best in Isaiah:

"No weapon formed against you will have any success."

Yet folks will continue to mosey on down that road to the bank and deposit all things toxic – bullying, jealousy, sabotage, and torment.

The projection – oh so palpable!

To them, having talent and skills that they don't have is like a garlic necklace on a vampire; they just can't handle it.

Folks project and fight what they are dissatisfied with in themselves. Perhaps mom and dad didn't pay them attention. A guy or gal they really liked went with the good-looking rival. Their spouse left them, or their siblings or children can't stand them. Better yet, THEY can't stand *themselves*.

Being nasty and disgusting will never increase your net-worth or self-worth. Why? Because that's just not how life goes. What you deposit you will withdraw – whether you want that withdrawal or not.

And you can take that to the bank!

SECTION III

EVERYTHING ELSE
IN BETWEEN

EARLY RISE

The smell of the fresh air
The quietude of the empty streets

My early morning rise
Today's new start and new opportunities
In my eyes

Can't wait to get started
Can't wait to execute good vibes
And best choices without question

Resolute!

As everyone else is sleeping
This head start guarantees my team and I
Over everyone else
Leaping

Throughout the day doing nothing but the best
Chaos and stress we'll leave to the rest

This early rise will serve us well
Already ten steps ahead at 4 AM

Can't you tell?

THE WORKPLACE

Quiet as it's kept
She did not accept
The way things currently stand
In this unsophisticated and wayward land

And so she dug in deep
With eyes on the prize
Strategies and plans
She did formalize

Always watching
Leaving an impression
Always ready
Unreservedly, without question

H.O.M.E.

Heavenly haven full of love
Open and spacious, cathedral ceilings above
Magical times ahead, very much is the case
Everything starts here, as this is our base!

TODAY'S CURRENT REALITY

Living our life in pictures
With all the trimmings and fixtures
Presenting the antithesis
Of what is real
Hoping our audience (if we in fact have one)
Does not see
That which we have concealed

A day in the life
A life in the day
Strolling through
Trying to make our own way

Rewriting history
So as not to quit
Hoping one day we make it
As we actively continue to fake it

TIME AWAY

Time away clears the mind
Relaxes
Refreshes
Releases by design

How fascinating it is
That the body inherently knows
It's in a new environment
Away from New York stress and anxiety

Quiet place
Time and space
To do what I love

Time to find a way
For "me" time headway
No angst or chaos

Hoping time stands still
To enjoy
Take it in
And just chill

NOT AS GOOD A FEELING

You plundered and pilfered
Uprooted and looted
And yet, you're still not happy
How do I know?
Your face and demeanor tell me so

Emaciated, agitated, disheveled
A shadow of your former self
I guess that land grab
Wasn't all it was cracked up to be
Was it?

That trail of destruction
You left behind
Showed the world who you really are
Insecure, deeply troubled and unkind

Missing the mark
Of what life's all about
Navigating your own world of
Mediocrity, duplicity, and self-doubt

Loving a good comeback story
The universe hopes
You will one day learn
Legitimate power, prestige
And responsibility
Are things that are earned

From the outside looking in
Everything looked appealing
Now in the thick of things
Coming to the realization
It's not as good a feeling

THE MOVEMENT OF REGRET

Dealt a blow
Not knowing where to go

Foundation rocked
Plans in disarray
Disorder running amuck
No new moves yet in play

Second guessing, rethinking
Why didn't I see that coming
This can't be happening
When in reality [pause]
Becoming a follower and believer
Is what's to blame

Guard down
Hopes up
'tis the season
Looking through rose-colored glasses
Ignoring all sense of reason

Asleep at the wheel
The route you took
From make-believe to reality
Your state of affairs now shook

Movements of regret
Good or bad
Lessons learned
That are ironclad

Movements of regret
Buyer's remorse
What's done is done
Let nature take its course

GO DEEPER

Our eyes are tickled
By the glitz and glamour
The red carpet
The picture taking
The superficial noise
The desired clamor

Intoxicated by the attention
We go all in
And fail to mention
We're one experience away
Broke and broken
As we continue to fall prey

Social media accounts flooded
With excess and opulence galore
Living "the life"

Have we lost the ability and desire
To go deeper?

When did shallowness and frivolousness
Become the standard
Of civilization?
Inherently we know that
All of this is fluff

ODE TO THE EXIT

It was good while it lasted
But, I AM OUT!
And to the rooftops
All I want to do is blast it

Shout from the bridge
Whisper it in the sea
Fantastic Voyage
Oh yeah, that's me!
Ode to the exit

When did it go from good to bad?
When did things go left?
When I saw the laziness, corruption
And, yeah, the blatant theft

Eyes wide open - eyes open wide
The cut and paste, who's on first
Repeat what's already been said approach
I'm taking it all in stride
Ode to the exit

The dysfunction
The ridiculousness
The pettiness
The games
It's no wonder folks are demanding
Massive, sweeping change

That trapped uncomfortable feeling
Never good for the soul
This wasn't just touching my work performance
It was affecting my very soul
Ode to the exit

Fast and furious
Slow and steady
It really doesn't matter
Because boy-oh-boy
I'm ready!

Final curtain call
Exiting, yes I must
On to bigger and better things,
Leaving this House of Cards in the dust
Ode to the exit

I'm out!

READ BETWEEN THE LINES

Attempts at being subversive
Your lot in life will never change
Increase your status
Or rearrange
What is already in place

The fast and furious
Set in stone
Settling in, taking the reigns
As you bemoan

Stuck in days gone by
Watching in disbelief
As the young, educated, and talented
Come in the night, as a thief

Devoid of professional presence
To those who make the decisions
Disorder, sabotage, and poison
Your only true provisions

Sly and sneaky your performance
A little league routine
Unable to dominate
This here business machine

THE CON

You weaseled your way
You got in
Hooray!

Now what?
Who knows!
Best be on your toes

You played your hand
Cunning, crafty, and crass
It's time to get to work
Or get thrown out on your ass

This environment is not
For the faint of heart
It comes with ebbs and flows
Refrain from cursing
And other bad behavior
Or you most certainly
Will come to blows

The Con is real
You proved to be a master
But for so many of us
All we really see is disaster

We look ahead with bated breath
For the Con we all will watch
Mr. Revolving Door smiling as he waits
On his belt another notch

YOU IN INFAMY

Right words, right tone
I will write you in infamy
The real, unadulterated you
A perfect symphony

Using my pen as my sword
And my mind as my shield
Opening the floodgates
To which I refuse to yield

The table I bring
About everything
You lack and you miss
Your lifelong blunders, abyss

As there is much to work with
It will be on point
No more white space available
As YOU fill up the joint

I LOVE WHAT I DO

I love what I do
Incompetence? Push through!
Getting the team back on track

Sifting through
Different temperaments and views
As I assess what it is that they lack

Strange sandbox indeed
As some my attention they need
While juggling this work and that

A feeling of accomplishment, yes
When we finally address
Everything that previously fell flat

SEE A NEED FILL A NEED

With blood, sweat, and tears
We come to this place
Anew, refreshed
This positive space

Eyes straight ahead
Wishing, hoping, doing
Talent at the ready
Working, helping, wooing

Many there are
All in need
Solutions delivered
As we proceed

To meet, greet, and treat
The masses we engage
Business doors wide open
As their problems we assuage

YOU KNOW WHO YOU ARE

someone saw fit
to move you up quick
with kitchen experience
no less

not learning
not knowing
a mess you are showing
and this, in disbelief
is your best

removed to the back
just deserts
you were smacked
but your plotting and planning's
still high

with any luck
with us
you are stuck
'cuz that rubbish will no longer fly

CALCULATED COINCIDENCE

(oxymoronic expressions of life)

What needs to come together
Does so on its own
Haphazardly deliberate
Grounded, steps unknown

Nothing by chance
Can it be so?
Accidentally on purpose
With plan and practice in tow

GONE

Good, dead, and gone
About time – so long!
No one will miss you one bit

Your tantrums and screams
Dashing our dreams
All we wanted to do was quit

You're giving her praise
But just yesterday
She was giving you hell on Earth

Now that she's dead
Finally quiet, instead
Her character you want to rebirth?

Get outta here with that
She was nothing but a rat
I don't do fake and phony

You lead, I'll follow
Take this hatred and swallow
As YOU started this acrimony

HOPE FULFILLED

Tears of joy
Relief in the streets
Hope fulfilled

Justice and accountability
Front and center
But is it?

And . . . what's next?
Was this a sacrifice to appease?
To move on? Forget?
Put the masses at ease?

Are those layers pulled
All the way back?
Or is it business as usual
As the deck remains stacked?

Wait and see
See and wait
Time reveals all
Mankind's inevitable fate!

A DAY IN THE DOLDRUMS

The pervasive undercurrent
Of insignificance
Triviality
Transgression
Mental assault
Boring predictability

The anti-creative abyss
Of contrived assimilation
Working hard
Or hardly working
The indecisive, untrained opportunist
Always shirking, always lurking

Disciplined professionals
Tired and frustrated
All because the productivity train
Is abruptly truncated

Riding the wave from place to place
Seeing first hand other countries
Outwork
Outperform, and
Outpace

This doldrums of a day
Is getting on my nerves
Will the real motivators and leaders
Please
Stand up and serve?

ANOTHER MEETING

Another meeting
And all is the same
Another meeting
And nothing has changed

We fall in line
With the status quo
The same old same old
Rigmarole

Why are we here
When it is clear
That effective change
We cannot steer?

Discipline and foresight
We do not have
With everyone focused on doing
A land grab

Mired in the ever-present kakistocracy
We leave this meeting
Not with more resources, clarity, and insight
But with a heightened realization
Of alarm, confusion, and plight

Up and down
In and out
Kick that can down the road
Is what it's all about

Up and down
Back and forth
This outrageous tragedy
Is, unfortunately, par for the course

MY TEAM IS BETTER THAN YOURS

You can't deny
That we work and get it done
Our hustle and heart
Are second to none

My team is better than yours!

We live and we breathe
Unmatched in our drive
To give our customers
A station environment that thrives

My team is better than yours!

In cleanliness and safety
In fast service, with grace
From Fulton and Broad
To Wall Street and Park Place

My team is better than yours!

Talent that far exceeds
The dreadful humdrum
Cooks and creatives
And one with a green thumb
Skills above and beyond all in one
As we collectively get the job done

My team is better than yours!

Formation in 1, 2, 3
For us in Zone 10
As we prepare for the next day
To do it all over again

Yeah

My team is *better* than yours!

UNSTOPPABLE

Your jealousy fuels me
Your envy fascinates me
Your passive-aggressiveness forces me
Your psychological projection educates me

For there is no alliance you can form
No action you can take
No side deal you can enter
No lie you can perpetrate
To slow me down
Or distract me
Or cause me to stop evolving

For
I AM spectacularly focused
And driven
An expert at problem solving

I AM UNSTOPPABLE!

THIS IS IT?

This cannot be it
Oh God, it is – I quit
This is not what I asked for back when

The 8-year-old me
Thrilled as can be
To be an adult, and get a job and then

Make money and have fun
The job, get it done
Having purpose and passion, it's true

The good and the bad
My resolve ironclad
As reality is a tad bit askew

KEEP GOING

That gap gets bigger
As you keep pulling the trigger
On your education, certifications, and skills

To enlighten and enhance
Deliberately, not by chance
To continue to eat and pay bills

But much more than that
In your preferred habitat
A measure of freedom to grow

To look to and thrive
Not simply survive
For the days we can pop the chateau

Just. Keep. Going.

UNTITLED

The routine stops
When there's loss of life
Things of no real value take a back seat
When there's grief and strife

This isn't new
We've seen this rerun
Never an appointed time
A young man with a gun

Business as usual
It just can't be
Human carnage
From a mass killing spree

Distance and social status
Shield no one from this human plight
The pariahdom and inhumanity
Glaringly downright

Taking the time to check
On coworkers, neighbors, and friends
Let's try again 'til we get it right
Compassion and empathy extend

THERE'S A THIEF IN OUR MIDST

Scumbags du jour
You cannot ignore
What's going on here, ceiling to floor

Opportunistic thief
Investigate – grief!
As YOU will do nothing at all

Our own Jesse James
Incredible as it is
Clueless you are to forestall

He is slick, he is sly
You cannot deny
Our disgust and unease with this place

Take what doesn't belong
Things, ideas and thoughts
Is what these people embrace

GROSSER THAN GROSS

Do more with less?!
I couldn't care less
If you get your bonus or not

I'm leaving at five
Don't worry, you'll survive
More important things, that's what I've got

Grosser than gross
You must be the most
Ugliest person I've met

Personality a brick
You're the best there is, trick
Wonder if powers that be feel regret

SHOWING 'EM HOW IT'S DONE

We moved with precision
Under your tutelage and vision
The ease, the flow
Of our actions and decisions

The skills and the talent
Oozing from within
A unit so tight
Never has there been

Skills and personalities
That fit like a glove
The arduous work
The labors of love

The togetherness and
Reciprocity of thought
Our best every day
Is indeed what we brought

With you at the helm
We knew we'd be okay
The camaraderie and support –
YOU were our mainstay

So, as we reflect
On work undeniably fun
We are happy to have been a part
Of showing 'em how it's done!

Heads held high
Eyes straight ahead
We thank you for all that you did
And all that you said

SECTION IV

ONE-LINERS

After 33 years, they thanked him with a pink slip.

THIS . . . this ain't it!

Create and become your own headline, mainline, and lifeline.

Stay as you are - flat out fabulous!

I AM the answer.

Thankfully, this disheveled mess

doesn't extinguish possibility and opportunity.

Let's embark on BIG.

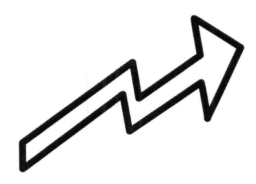

I have  books

in me.

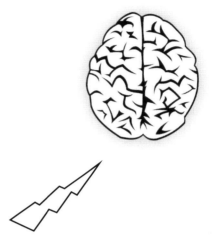

You are forever seared in my brain.

Today's forecast is cloudy with a 90% chance of stupidity.

Listen for the silence, you'll learn a great deal.

You have to subtract to add.

If you're going to lie to me, please put some effort into it.

If the goal is to run your operation

like a circus-style comedy show,

by all means,

put the crown on the clown.

STOP, look, and leave.

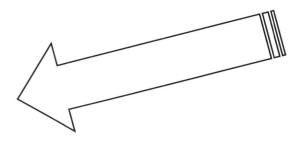

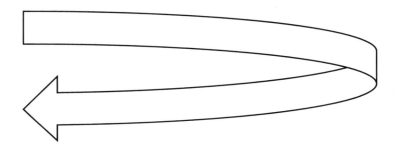

Sometimes you have to go outside

to get in on the inside.

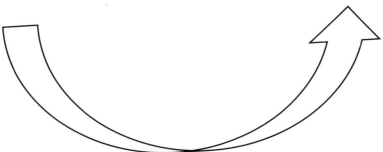

A genuine smile is the antidote to many problems.

You cannot erase reality.

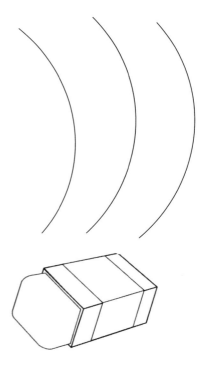

Your teeth and eyes tell the story.

The phenomenon that is . . .

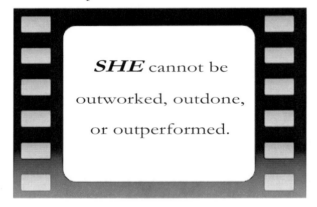

SHE cannot be
outworked, outdone,
or outperformed.

Take note of the timing, temperature, and tempo.

They're weary, she's wired!

I can do this in my sleep.

You do better when I do better.

I do better when you do better.

Re Start

If it doesn't materialize go back to the drawing board.

If you don't *see* the standard, *become* the standard.

Watching the undisciplined and untrained

in complete stupefaction.

Acknowledging and accepting the remarkably empty and vaingloriousness of one's service

is the first step to bigger and better things.

Bedlam and pandemonium are to the incompetent and unqualified,

as a hand is to a glove.

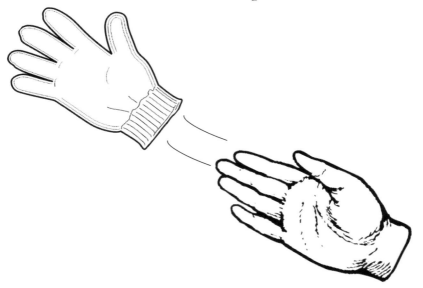

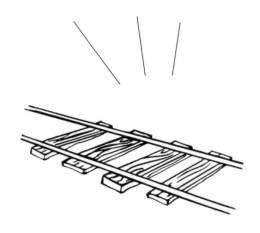

My level of disquietude continues to heighten as I see

train wreck,

after train wreck,

after train wreck.

Although you are identical twins,
the green-eyed monster does not look good on you.

Why is it that the mediocre, scantily skilled employee

never experiences imposter syndrome

but, at times,

some outstanding, go-to employees do?

Try
brightening
day of
who can give
nothing in

up the
someone
you
return.

SECTION V

SOMETHING LIKE THIS . . .

JOB ADVERTISEMENT, REALER THAN REAL

At what point do we let go of the lilies and daffodil-like verbiage in these job notices? How do you expect employees to be honest and truthful when you are quite the opposite with them, straight out the gate? How do you attempt to quell the high turnover and lack of productivity? Hmmmm. What would a realer than real job advertisement even look like?

Perhaps it would look something like this . . .

ASSISTANT MANAGER

Location: Wherever we feel like sending you. (Are you up for the challenge?)

Job Details: $40 an hour – Fuller than full time w/ no additional compensation. (We do, however, believe that your self-actualization and belonging needs will be met, as we need you on the team)

Qualifications

- Bachelor's degree in any field. (We really don't care about the field because this only applies to those applicants who have no chance of getting this job)

- Work authorization (Required, unless you know someone on the inside)

Full Job Description

Act as a magician, psychologist, no commonsense whisperer, and gatekeeper of obstinate frontline and eggshell ego higher-ups. Manage dysfunction without making the status quo feel like you're changing things and making them look bad. Decipher and process unintelligible reports, navigate a communication minefield, and stifle all discernment and power of reason. Figure it out, even though you will not be properly trained – and don't mess up the revenue!

Desired Skills

Proactive approach to problem-solving and strong follow-through habits (although your efforts and hard work will be in vain)

Provide courteous and efficient service to external and internal customers (although some of our customers lack etiquette almost as if they were born in a barnyard)

Perform day-to-day activities such as scheduling inspections (although once the inspections have been completed, the findings will stay in queue in the database, in perpetuity)

Service-based attitude - although coworkers and the culture are anything but

TAKING BACK OUR BRAIN POWER

Job elimination, being replaced, and the dumbing-down of society, make the case for why we should not invest more time, money, and energy in artificial intelligence and other software. How do we put that genie back in the bottle? What would that kind of send-off even look like?

Perhaps it would look something like this . . .

Dear Artificial Intelligence & Company,

You have been nothing but a poisoned chalice, a trojan horse of sorts, as you've convinced me, not only to rely on you, but to stay in this abusive relationship. In this short period of time that we have been together, I have outsourced a good portion of my thinking ability to you, to my complete and lasting detriment.

Without realizing it at the time, I unwittingly put the best computer system on the planet – yes, my brain - in hibernation and storage to some extent, albeit temporarily. The depth and breadth of inactivity has been so intellectually life-threatening that I have moments of disbelief when I ask certain questions. Questions I should already know the answer to and methods I should already know, to arrive at the answers that I need.

By design or otherwise, you have contributed to the widening gap between the haves and the have-nots. The inability to calculate and discern problems, apply critical thinking skills, or know how to spell or form basic sentences has decreased my chances of success.

But don't you worry! I fully intend to make you unfashionable and expendable like the gadgets and technologies of centuries past. Because there is no piece of technology that is more energy-efficient, brilliant, creative, and self-sustaining than my brain, as it is wonderfully made.

Sincerely,

Paying Attention to What Is Happening

THE DECLINE OF BUSINESS ETIQUETTE

Etiquette blunders have skyrocketed in recent years. So much so that in some groups it is the new normal. Is this because the workplace landscape is changing to a more informal atmosphere? Or could it be that the stress and anxiety that have plagued us since the pandemic, have altered our DNA and how we comport ourselves with others? Or is it that, with some of us, the uncivil monster has been lying dormant for so long, waiting to come out and wreak havoc? Seems like there is a case for a grand jury indictment against the uncivil monster within. But what would that even look like?

Perhaps it would look something like this . . .

INCIVILITY OFFENSE

The grand jury charges that on or about February 1, 2020 at New York, NY, in the Eastern District of New York, Jane Doe defendant herein, with the intent to cause discord, disruption, chaos, and cessation of teamwork and revenue-generating activities, did take from the persons or presence of others, to wit, (victims), by force, intimidation, deviancy, actions, behaviors, and mindset, that were developed and nurtured internally, that is, an ungentlemanly deportment and unpolished character, all in violation of Title 8, Universal Business Etiquette Code, Section 1914:

COUNT 1: Felony Rudeness
COUNT 2: Criminal Impersonation (of a Professional)
COUNT 3: Aggravated Moral Turpitude
COUNT 4: Felony Unprofessional/Discourteous Email Messaging
COUNT 5: Aggravated Microaggression & Hostile Work Environment Contributor
COUNT 6: Criminal Dress & Grooming in the First Degree

DISDAINED REMEMBRANCE

You have to fight that natural desire to be a rotten human being. Otherwise, you're just going to make yourself and those around you miserable. And who of us wants to live a miserable existence? Why would anyone in their right mind want to consciously be unpleasant to other people? How would your family even transpose that kind of life to your obituary or funeral brochure?

Perhaps it would look something like this . . .

IN DISDAINED REMEMBRANCE

JANE DOE

Disliked Sister, Ex-wife, and Mother leaves behind 2 estranged adult children, Noah and Liam; 3 ex-husbands, Oliver, Cecil and Chad; and a host of dejected staff who are indifferent about Jane's death, as they know it would be socially unacceptable
to be joyful and in good spirits in this time of
what can only be described as change and loss.

Jane thoroughly enjoyed cracking the whip and holding people back, both personally and professionally, from bigger and better opportunities. From her family to her staff, their smiles immediately extinguished when she entered the room. They will not miss witnessing Jane browbeat others in their presence, nor will they miss hearing her gossip endlessly on the phone.

In lieu of flowers, funeral home personnel request donations be made to the following organizations:

Humanity Rising
The Work Wellness Institute
The National Association of People Against Bullying
The National Federation of Families

The funds that would have originally been used for Jane's service will be divvied up and sent to all those whom she hurt and tormented over the years, for therapy and other treatments.

EXPRESS YOURSELF

EXPRESS YOURSELF

EXPRESS YOURSELF

EXPRESS YOURSELF

EXPRESS YOURSELF

EXPRESS YOURSELF

ACKNOWLEDGMENTS

Thank you,

Ms. Wells, Renee, and Toscha

ABOUT THE AUTHOR

Sandréa Flowers is a writer, thinker, and lifelong businesswoman from both sides of the aisle – corporate and small business ownership. After more than a decade of quietly observing her surroundings and penning her experiences, Sandréa compiled her first poetry collection, *Gotta Be a Better Way Volume 1*. She is the author of *Market Your Career Like You Mean It* and *Manage THIS! A Day in the Life of Control, Influence, and Chaos*. She also owns several other copyrighted works and trademarks. In her spare time, Sandréa enjoys learning, spending time with family, and managing her self-care.